The Law of Poetry

Also by MTC Cronin

Poetry

Zoetrope – we see us moving

the world beyond the fig

Everything Holy

Mischief-Birds

Bestseller

Talking to Neruda's Questions
[Respondiendo a las Preguntas de Neruda (Spanish/English)]
[Controcanto ~ Il Libro Delle Domande di Neruda (Italian/English)]

My Lover's Back ~ 79 Love Poems

The Confetti Stone and other poems

beautiful, unfinished ~ PARABLE/SONG/CANTO/POEM

<More or Less Than> 1-100

The Ridiculous Shape of Longing ~
New & Selected Poems (Macedonian/English)

The Flower, the Thing

Notebook of Signs (& 3 Other Small Books)

Our Life is a Box. / Prayers Without a God

How Does a Man Who is Dead Reinvent His Body?
The Belated Love Poems of Thean Morris Caelli (co-written with Peter Boyle)

Irrigations (of the Human Heart) ~ Fictional Essays on
The Poetics of Living, Art & Love

The World Last Night [metaphors for death]

in possession of loss

Essays

Squeezing Desire Through a Sieve ~ Micro-essays on
Judgement & Justice

The Law of Poetry

MTC Cronin

Puncher & Wattmann

First published in 2015
Published by Puncher and Wattmann
PO Box 441
Glebe NSW 2037
http://www.puncherandwattmann.com
puncherandwattmann@bigpond.com

National Library of Australia
Cataloguing-in-Publication entry:

Cronin, M.T.C.
The Law of Poetry

ISBN 9781922186614
I. Title.
A821.3

Cover design by Tim Cronin
Printed by McPhersons Printing Group

The writing of this book was assisted by grants from the Ian Potter Cultural Fund.

This project has been assisted by the Australian Government through the Australia Council, its arts funding and advisory body.

Australian Government

Australia Council for the Arts

for
Regina Graycar
&
Dirk Meure

true laws aren't manmade
they make man

The Law

The fool still here in it jumps up.
A rapid and lively dance like a hieroglyph by night.
The gods are hanging from its lifted feet.
They fizz and splutter.
Little fox toenails clatter like beginnings.
Like stars skittering up the discs of its spine.
The soles of its feet are black and cracked.
Its shadow's *en route* to no companion.
But its heart is a dance stopped.
It is its own death it does not notice.
Although the stars wobble like unworthy souls.
And the gods it makes fly out like blows.
The fool in it jumps up.
The fool in it jumps up.
But it's all just fizz and splutter.

The Law Of A Thing

There is two kinds of everything.

A chicken stuffed with snow
and a chicken not stuffed with snow.

These are not two kinds of a thing.

The Law Of Abandonment

The sole law of abandonment, like the law of love,
is to be without return and without recourse.
Jean Luc Nancy

Letting go!
Pointing the gun at the mirror!
Finally, believing in life!

The Law Of Absolutes

Each poem, each number is an instantaneous absolute.
A lesson in sobriety and heroism.
                    Octavio Paz

Closely aligned to the idea of halves

There is one half and there is the other

Life is instead of nothing

And though there is that expression

Life is slipping away

It never abates

Use it in the bedroom

Use it on the battlefield

To step around that music on the ground

To withstand the light

And to withstand the dark

For it becomes absolutely certain

Some things eventuate

Some appear to be this or that

Like the forbidden

Or where the poor will live

But all is collapsible

The apple into the horse

And the horse into the apple

One half into the other

A sleeping child's hand slipped

Into the frequent destination of Heaven

The Law Of Another Universe

What will the good Father in Heaven say
to the local judge if he do not solve this problem?
A little two-pointed smile and – pouff –
the law is changed into a mouthful of phrases.
                    William Carlos Williams

What really happens in heaven?
Is it part of our universe or another?
Lyotard suggests you cannot establish
the reality of the universe because
the universe is the object of an idea.
Can you establish the reality of a smile?
Who is to judge if he or she really smiled?
It is not God who judges but God
who wants us to judge.
When we do we feel God's smile
and know the smile has its origin in fear.
An act of submission between two parties.
The animal grin.
Minus the anger, plus pleasure.
And what really happens when you smile?
A new universe is created where the laws
fall away and an idea is reality?
Who is to judge if not us.
Crying as we laugh and holding retribution
above our heads as if it was an umbrella.
Does it rain in heaven?

The Law Of Ants

We watch them like those Gods
looking down from above in those old movies

They move and we are still
in our larger movements

If one suddenly grows and turns human
we are shocked

As if it could be like us
Until we remember we are Gods

and crush it
and reassume our height

and size

We bury the body in the backyard
and don't answer any questions

until we have spoken
to our lawyers

looking out at us from the corner of their eyes
Shifty like in those old movies

We would like to clean up this latest war
by upending the birdbath

but during our time in prison
over a million ants

tunnel to freedom

The Law Of Babies

This is a closed law
which relies on no others

Dawn again
and the priority that lifts itself
outside its genre

It is a law in which all things are seen
in their approach
to the body

Flesh before time and time
bearing only scent to the dream

Oh! and movement –
that shrug to life

Don't make lists here
or proscribe how this is to be that

It is true that the bitter is the sweet
You only really become
what you are

The Law Of Balance
(or 'The Imbalance')

In poetry, evening and twilight balance perfectly.
Mystery balances with any word you choose to weigh it against.
Poetry, however, puts the whole world out of whack.
When you read it you drift up or down
while everything else goes in the opposite direction.
If you read 'There's no dust that isn't honest'
the dust from your feet ends up in your head.
When you read 'womanliness', your hands,
which had been empty, are suddenly full of breasts.
If the poet says to you 'I wish to teach the wind to speak', well,
the wind stops blowing long enough for you to fall about laughing.
What's needed to even things back up is a poet who can take
the poetic punishment out of evening and twilight.
Such a person will have no regard for beauty
and a thoroughgoing disregard for how things might be put.
Such a poet knows that there are no strange ways
to say 'I love you' and that the orange-red-purple glow
that accompanies the particular time under discussion
violates more, much more, than a sense of the well-ordered.
As you might have figured, you are not allowed to gush
and any short or long sigh which signifies your appreciation
will only show you up as some kind of critic.
After this it's a pity you can't just die in your sleep.
The balance then would be reset until the next arbiter
of good taste comes along with eyes wide
in amazement at truly seeing the world in all its glory (read,
only the bits that stick out because somebody else

has already attached a formula to them).

And the balance is reset because for you, with death,

there is no twilight, only the impossible sky of another realm

and a reaction that remains unknown.

José Touches His Toes
(Laws Behind Bars)

José's smooth bum
leans up against the cold wall
Tight pants
go all the way to the floor
And José says
"It feels like a cunt
It really does"
And the man looks
at José's smooth face
and small hands
and tight smile and says
"I ain't never had
a woman in prison,
you sayin' I should
start now?"
Tight pants
fall all the way to the floor
And José touches his toes
and says
"Unnecessary,
just look on it as a
situational constraint."

Big Law (2)

Big law with a big buckle and a big hat
and an invisible buckle and an invisible hat
and a silver buckle and a pointy hat
and a hat with an insignia (if you like)

Big hatless big law with boots and all
and hands with no fingerprints and a vice
and long arms and longer arms and the longest
and a scapegoat which you keep as a pet

Big brother big motherfucker big daddy law
whose children are all born from a barren womb
whose only direction is your own —
you are not a father!

Our father pointed and then left us
where our decision was to be formed:
whether to decide or whether to make it
another big fat law

The Blackest Law

for Johannes Beilharz

That you do not allow the stars to begin.
That you hold the objects that make you crazy.
That you think of absolute necessity.
That you reconstruct the impulse.
Doing the few hours of a morning.
Safely dead.
Forerunning the night.
What kind of motive do you have?
To make your soul cry out as if mortal?
To show your face worthlessness by its own look?
To leave?

You do it all to discover if the blackest law is white.
But what you need to know is decided by what you know.
See the brightest orange flower.
In the night.
Nothing touches your eyes...
Gently with darkness.
Darkness always feels closer than light.

The Law Of Blue Eyes

is the most simple
one is blue
the other is blue
no room for the legitimacy
of a single cloud
in this jurisprudence
of border flowers where
voluntary bees are giving
up honey to the sunrise
(though in the cities
we only see the sun
on the walls
all heat rushing into
the retreat of stone)
and in this green-suited
day her eyes burn with old
images and when
she is angry her words
are with me and
clear

everflowing the fountain
of no discernible
change

The Law Of Bones

Cement too, dies;
our children become those we once enslaved;
we live in the clothes, eating the food,
of those long dead whom we bear
no relation to; the balconies crack
and fall from our houses.

How close to the revolution we always
come and how we divide up the years
to elect new lives worth cheering to;
over and over we are dragged to
the oases and stand, hands pressed
to the gates of the wilderness.

We write
the fiction of immorality, the fiction of the rose;
with the knife savour flesh; with the gun
our distance from death.
We toil, we assemble, we hear the colours
burning behind us.

Where is necessity on any day
between the bone forming and the bone
decaying? Do we fear what we suspect
or do we fear what we believe?
What, when what we understand
means nothing?

Each of you, do you think
there is a shining page where you will find
all your inspiration, words unstatued,
sounding not echoing and supposing
the space, the wanton, imaginary space,
surrounding death?

Well writing is collaboration
with the wilderness that is *in* our bones
and how many other bones occupy
this place in which, still working, we gather
up the bricks and block the hole, in which
we create and recreate happiness, anything.

The Law Of Books

is subordinated to the law
of the text in blood
a text which speaks
your mouth full of bones
your mouth of exposed bones
what we wish
to keep among us
what we wish
to send among us
and all the time
it seems like gathering
and as if it is never too far
to go for beauty
yet even as we achieve silence
and lay our words down in it
the sound is still there
pursuing our lips
to get back in
to get back in and find
our throats our chests
our brains its house
you think it's the story you tell
but it is really the dream
pulling you into
its mouth

Boundary Laws
(Fearing The Void)

for Peter Goodrich & Dean Kiley

The boundaries of facts
can differ from the boundaries
of what is interesting.

The boundaries of the chair
coincide with the boundaries
of classical works on rhetoric.

The boundaries of stories
hide behind a brick wall
and ambush you *en masse*.

The boundaries of the banal
are a recurring nightmare
filled with identikit faces.

The boundaries of dreams
have no openings (like what
shape is thought to represent).

The boundaries of originality
are in reality about
accomplice identification.

The boundaries of the rose
are as widely spread
as a woman's legs.

The boundaries of breath
though uncontained
are always dwindling.

The boundaries of the moment
say there is no need to decide
now – Judgment is for Jupiter:

Because the orange fell
into the hand it was juicy
in the mouth.

The boundary of the orange
is the mouth though it may be
only a random encounter.

And the boundaries of this
are too marginal or incidental
to form a deliberative account.

Contrarily

any immense rumour
has the boundaries
of a penetrating kiss

and those of the kiss end
where does the banquet.
Each and every boundary

prevents emptiness flowing
into what is encapsulated
by the skull.

For similar purposes
all the brain's nothingness
easily permeates most boundaries.

The notable exception
is the boundaries of thought
which thus locked in

fear the void.

The Law Of The Box

Is that we understand it.
That we find it satisfying.
That we tell our children the box.
Both dismantled and assembled.
It is close to the sun and the moon.
The cube that may be hollow or filled.
It is close to the terror
                           of owning a body.
Recognizing what is before consideration.

The Law Of Broccoli

is like the law of yellow flowers
going to seed
you can eat it raw
or put it in a jar
like a bunch
it is so chaste
yet lush
it gets me all bothered
the flowers are like
beautiful little narcotics
and I count them
all afternoon
the broccoli is so green
that it leads me
to the end of analogy
where everything is sleepy and still
and quite
unconvincing

The Law Of The Burden

They don't let you go
through real life by yourself.
Blood squeaking like a pair of shoes,
bread too, because an angel can smell
a drop of humanity
in the newest, most infinous, void,
in the most populous named world
amidst the screams screamed against
the aggravation of the curse placed
by the god other to the god
who is not yet named.
That is our burden,
knowing and calling to God.
Such faith takes us to the place
where thinking stops
so our thoughts
can be piled and sacked
and raised to our backs.
And those finished thoughts *are* God.
Have you ever tried going through
life with God on your back?
It's not like carrying a cello
or a double bass.

The Law Of Catching The Worm

This law's got you by the bright and earlys
The sun comes up in the elevator
you swallowed and out of pure debt
the world goes to work in your head

The worm has a bit of unexpected advice —
Sack it and all its cultures! and if you catch
my drift you'll find you're not even
your own boss and the prize is never one

It's a bit like designing the fractal that cracks
out of your birthing egg says the worm
turning to see what you're up to
since the notion of success got debunked

The Temporary Gallows
(The Law Of Cause & Effect)

The length of the rope is not right.

Jerking like an animal lost in its skin.

The weight of the body is not right.

A light or heavy eden?

The animal is exhausted.

As they watch from a casual distance.

All their knowledge in what they built.

Dismantled.

The crime caused a riot.

All their eyes left their dead.

The length of the rope was not right.

Covering the same distance as fear.

Chance's Permissive Laws

Not that your heart resumes beating after the sneeze.

Not that the body rations its blood.

Not that the meteor is beauty too close.

Not that the eye socket waits for the arrival of scars.

Not that tears stop the flow of crying.

Not that the moon is as frail as a fingernail.

Not that memory is like elastic stretching back to hurtle you.

Not that the disappearing sound of the forest is our gasp.

Not that all steps are towards death.

Not that the real name of the cover-up is life.

But that you allow all these things.

That you give them a chance to destroy you.

That you afford them the chance to let you live.

The Law Of Chaos

a slow-flying insect
pulling me into slow motion
slowing my mind
growing wings

where is the story of this?
and how slowly I read the marks of another
there is much I suspect
such as how to resay things like vision...

and I look for you
in what you dreamed
in your tiredest moment
in the authenticity of chaos

and of narration: *live the soul*
disorderly and forever

The Law Of The Child, Lost

that faithfulness of reality
identified by the poet
on an ordinary evening
is recorded here

above, was a bird
with a thousand small zebras
on its back
black and white feathers
racing the sky's even field
from winning blue
to infinite white

the child ran ahead —
children are always doing that
it is the only way
they can look back at you —
they find history that way
and the origin of the future
which they rush towards
as if hearing it craven and ringing
like an unanswered phone
buried deep in the unfair earth

~•~

Never to the sound of my voice,
turning her head
with as yet no contemplation

of mind without body,
I remember my child's smile

it is only a small part
of the smile of the woman
who today
comes through my door
yet with the familiarity
of so many days and nights
I bequeathed to her
and which now pass
under her own hands
and across those same lips

'The Laws Of The Communicant Clouds'

after Vicente Huidobro

Historically, I am not welcomed.
This is a point of differentiation among people.
A hair-worm has been known to utter the cry of a horse.
The whatness of anything is all that is dutiful to it.
Clouds see what there is yet still move like traffic.
Beneath them men search with a new tool.
It tells them what is deep in the ground and what it's made of.
They are like pigs after truffles.
What's so bad about being lost forever?
All to pieces and if we don't have a toad, we need a toad!
Any ghost is worth telling this to.
Being unknown I urge them.
Throw all your tools into the wound of your mother's chest.
As well the knife that opened her.
The shades of clouds discharge the sweet brightness.
What name will I sign giving authenticity to this falseness?
A side-wind that took out the battle-wall of a millennium?
I am welcomed finally as the shadow casting another.
Markless.
History has the cloudy eyes of a washed-up fish.
Surveillance is always naïve.

The Law Of Concrete

All around me
concrete walls of the house

In my hand
a wild strawberry

Uneasily red and fading
to the pink smell of a captured fruit

Trying to be less red
than the imaginary heart

Talking louder
than the heart of a small beast

And
as on children's feasts and celebrations

The concrete looks kindly
on our two breaths

The Law Of Contraries

for Lajos Kassák

The Law of Contraries
is not contrary
to what it isn't

Its aim is to outlaw
its own existence
(contrarily enough)

The absence
of a Law of Contraries
is not contrary to this law

This law
is the only contrary thing
it permits

'The Little Law
That Controls A Sponge'

after Fabio Morabito

Of all hands, only the hand of a child
has absolutely no fear of the sponge.
How to deduce this? Well, the sponge
is about the art of deduction and will
reduce whatever its hearts swallow
whereas a child, small, intent, caring
yet without concerns has no fear at all
of reduction and what it is related to.
Children, with their numerous arms
and exploding mouths, unaccountable
silences and magical abilities with facts
are masters in the arts of the sponge.
They know that the moment exists as
time does not and hold onto whatever
they can in it. Already moving, always
changing yet in their own eyes staying
the same, they take more and more
while convincing inside the disguise
of need that they will do a better job
of almost anything that is asked them
if only their light and spacious thoughts
are constantly filled with enthusiasm.
A child is well aware that the little law
which controls the sponge is derived
from derivation. A little person, still
close to the source, needs no memory,
no canvas, no story or surface to put

this in or on. Children, like all sponges,
simply follow, simply take and break
everything down, growing heavier
and lighter and heavy again having
regard always to what is given and to
what from them is wrung. If left they
will soak, accumulate things at random,
and in each and every end they must
grow dirtier and decay from a surfeit
of 'to do' and 'done' and 'do again'. So
much taken inside is eventually more
than any cosmos can accommodate —
pathways close down and soft edges
crumble onto the floor of what will be
forgotten and therefore may as well be
Heaven. To the memory this is known
as nostalgia, how the adult remembers
childhood. To the sponge it is the point
of giving in for there's only so much
that can be held and only so much also
which can be let go. A sponge becomes
useless as a sponge and a child useless
as a child. That's why we get new ones.

The Law Of Crimes

Unsolved crimes tend to remain unsolved...
                              Comment from a newspaper article.

of course I'm lying said the man who climbed
and picked the highest lemon from the tree
said the drummer who did not drum
said the woman eating shit from a spoon
chirped the bird guiding men to honey
clucked the pork chicken and the old lady
out of practice with the poor
lying said the saint in today's labour market
said three burning stars trying to catch sight
of themselves in the mirror through
a barely opened window
also claimed the young girl ending love
and another bottling the spices of hell
and we too said the self-professed
who could be anything they chose
and as well the authors of their own reason
I was lying said the grandfather
pretending to be water issuing from rock
and so was I said the book
which was the sum of all books

all who spoke claimed to speak falsely
and the dignity around them
held no lies or contests and all in the end
were happy that unsolved crimes
tend to remain unsolved... until
it is alleged the dreamer asked:
what of the solved; were they, then,
ever unsolved?

The Law Of Darkness?

Can darkness enter
or only light?

There is no law of darkness.

Darkness
was always in here.

Before law. Before light.

Darkness
which does not visit

but inhabits.

Which governs all
the laws of light.

The Law Of Death

Alters the time of my birth.
All four legs of the chair support this.
Shadows overlap until there is nothing
but shadows.
Wild honey mixed with ash.

My name sops up darkness.
The only one with a face
at the masked ball.
Lungs happy with smoke.
The dropped fardel.

Even the moon knows the end
of the chapter.
Death, the most moral of our ideas.
How brave to live by it.
Death, the greatest duty of life.

The Law Of Deduction
(or 'Was Princess Youssoupoff Ravished?')

What do you think
If this poem is
As short as her skirt?

The Law Of Descriptions

Tired of the old descriptions of the world,
The latest freed man rose at six and sat
On the edge of his bed. He said,
                              "I suppose there is
A doctrine in this landscape. ..."
                    Wallace Stevens, 'The Latest Freed Man'

from his own standpoint

he enjoyed a happy life

of crime and laziness

not in the eye of the war

nor in the cold belly of the whale

not in the path of sticks and stones

but rather lawless in a red shirt

with opinions and writing poems

about his dreams

he saw ideology

before opening his eyes

and said:

'the way I say this

so that what I say

will not be questioned'

The Law Of Desire

What is worthy of desire?

A man needs one woman or fifty men.

There is a shark in the blood.

The best prey is living.

A man hunts forward.

The soft wind convinces us.

Desire is like the emptiness of a chair.

Adventure undoes adventure.

The women never rise.

All lines are one.

I am the mother of a corpse.

The Law Of Destruction

The Law
does not like us to destroy
but we are all
covered in dirt
from the holes we have dug

And your face is changing
growing thinner and younger
than it was
at the beginning
of my dream

You have ruined
my face
the one I came to you with
and held up
for kissing

And will someone come
and hold you responsible?
For what I feel —
For what I don't feel —
My unused perfume and comb!

The Law Of Direction

Direction is in us
North to West
The way that causes most pain
The least
Ask a bird
Who flies through East
On the way to enchantment
A new sun
Or a cat over the railway tracks
On its way to the past
The Old Town
I turn toward you at 3am
Please show me love
Without its skin
Direction is in us
The light filling the tunnel
A twinkle of doubt
The tunnel oblivious
Going South

The (Disorderly) Law Of Dreams

This could have been

The law of owls
Or
The law of the body in space
Or
The law of bitter thoughts

But

As only the dreamer knows
The dreamer's dreams
This soul whispers
Its immodest story
Only when no-one listens

Listen –

Blood rushing the tunnel of your breath

The silence
Of an appeased wind

The Law Of Ducks

their influence on you is underestimated
all that quacking yellow rubber
bathtubs and beaks

I saw this one once
peering at me over a corrugated iron fence
like an unblinking cardboard cut-out

and it was
staring from bloodless lungs
so *represented* that it could only be looking

for nothing restless nor anything
but a pencil drawing of the pale blue pond
under the impure silence

of a high moon
for this contention I have the full support
of my subconscious not to mention

photographic proof

The Law Of Ears And Also Things Close

If sound waves carry on to infinity,
where are their screams now?
                    Anne Michaels, *Fugitive Pieces*

sound as close as my ears
and upon the side of the green hill
a lace of seagulls
unravelling its own pattern
and then no birds
just shadows of birds

small thoughts
black thoughts
that woman and her child
will die in the next war
a new law
means we take it seriously

and they still die…
and of luck?
the black sky laughs
and asks what possible exceptions
could you have to the moon?
right and wrong

behind the veil of the sky
listening to the argument
of six moral philosophers

standing on a pin
and my sound-filled body
is the point of access

falling it rings out
heavy as a rock
in this avalanche
as before the cliffs
black foam rises uncertainly
towards the dust in my head

The Law Of Eggs

What came first,
the egg or the law?

Every Law

Every law presumes ignorance.
And tombs.
All are artless.
Humping the limits of a thing.
Turning simultaneously.
Both for and against the clock.
Order thriving on disorder.
Cornering desire.
Indulged by justice.

To live without them.
Don't be responsible for too much.
Because you must be responsible.
For every thing.
The law never made lays down this.
And you can't remove it with any tool.

The Law Of Evidence

No one knows what the laws are. That there are laws
we know, by the daily burnings, if nothing else.
                              Anne Carson, 'TV Men: Sappho'

1. Intellectual

In our fireplace we are burning wood —
300 years old and embedded with square-headed nails
and its own splitting, the gentle and slow rub of flames
along its straight back rising orange and upright
as if drawn toward some higher place that awaits
all courage.

And when she speaks, her lips curve upwards.

This fire is brave to love *this* wood
because other fire has preceded it, the planks
collected from a house round the corner
which burned but not
to the ground.

And he looks away.

I will call it the second burning
and this burning, evidence,
that intellectual conquest
of time.

And ash? he says, and misses her smile, what is to be born.

And ash, she says, evidence of evidence,
of what came before,
no more –

2. *Litigious*

Daughter is derived from the verbal root, *duh*, to milk.

Is this burnt stick, wood or bone?

He claimed on the one hand to be the dead girl's father
yet while she lived he denied paternity.

Do we have an expert to tell us
at what temperature bone turns to ash?

She is the dead girl's mother, that one sitting there,
not smiling.

Duh?

What is being described here bears no resemblance
to what really happened.

The moment of love?
The conflagration?

The house stood for three hundred years.
Her eyes were a colour none could agree on.

Does anyone here know
what these questions are trying to elicit?

The term, *father*, is rarely applied to animals.

3. *Poetically*

… and she said, my belly.
And he said, could have been anyone.

Her eyes are like the man's
her mother smiled at
before she was born.

Is green just a species
of blue?

What is meant
by animal?

The fire in her eyes is like that
in the man's who looked away
from her mother's smile.

Daughter means derived
from another, could have been anyone.

The Law Of Explanations

We need not live in a world we do not like...
                    Rodrigo Crenshaw – creation of Richard Delgado

parts of a turtle distinguished as turtle's parts –
calipash & calipee – yet I have built a turtle
from becoming friendly with the idea
and the constancy of my mind

(for turtles); similarly

those who wait through suffering for what survives
have always seen the rain, the wind, the snow
the empty plate, the dry cup, the hard face
and have known them wet and cold

and hard; know

that suffering survives like your hand on the end
of your arm and that the rest is life where
the hand works – and this means...?
do not wait for anything to end –

belly & shell; there is

every need for accuracy in love and we are all
helpless before the explanation of another –
my turtle does not live in a world it does
not like and loves to poke its head

out; (into the sun)

The Law Of Facts

Death is not a discrete event
that is easily identifiable.
                              Charles M Kester

testimony seen through the window
becomes grey in the rain

and white in the snow

and blue as a bandit sky
thinking it is hiding from the weather

when it *is* that

as loud as the loud-singing moon
up-close and faceless

as quiet as glass

moreover
shock may not be

and the smile may be the fear

it evolved from
over five years and five million

and seen through the window from another

the scene of death is redeemable
as sleep

of the argument

as theatre
and of the kiss

as greeting not farewell

the experience of honey
makes honey sticky and sweet

perception

embodied in perception
and though our stories are what is accurate

is knowledge of blood stains

different
to knowledge of love?

I Can Feel Law

I can feel law.
It's like London was
or the triangle edges
of our monolith
down South.

I can feel it
when the words cease
and when they speak
with small
and suspicious tongues.

Law feels like
myth that's gone
a bit hard
or how it feels
pretending to beg.

You can feel it
when you read something
over and over
and still don't have
bits of life in you.

In fact the only time
you can't feel law
is when
you can feel everything else
properly.

Of course law
makes sure
that it comes carefully
between
you and all those things.

Law makes sure
you can always feel it
and that it feels like
a timely warning
about regret.

It's either that
or the kind of feeling
you have
when you miss out
on 100lbs of free god.

The Law Of The Fine Line
& The Law Of The Thin Line

Knowing the difference
Relies on the methodology of neither.

Life & Death are in the same boat
But Lonely & Alone is quite different.

Understanding, however, what the thin line is
Can often be a fine line.

The fine line, on the other hand, is much too fine
To be subjected to any external measurement.

Meanwhile, as far as the law is concerned,
Subtle distinctions and opposites have fallen in love.

How long it will last might to varying degrees depend
On more than their toleration of difference.

The Law Of The First Venus

I have fallen in love
With paradox
There is no history
Because of unity
The way her arms so naturally
Bind me
There is no place even
To start counting

Yet against her thrilling wall
I lean
She is unscaleable!
My arrows shoot to the stars
Yet note is taken
They reach somewhere
Just below the height
Of her lovely belly

She is the first Venus always
To be approached
By such laughable Reason
On the specious surface
Little draw
What I write
With my true love
On her willing wall

Like this
She is never finished
The big sleeping girl
The hiding doll
The twitch
Of the dreaming leg
Never actualized
Not even in death

See her coming up
Singing cups of tea today
Introducing
The line to the curve
Its sneaky self
What a beautiful Queen of Sheba!
I'm to be her toad
Her platter of fruit!

And I have fallen in love
With paradox
There is no history
Because of life
The way her arms move
So naturally to bind me
There is no place even
To begin

The (Second) Law Of The Game

I must tell you of my felony.
It is, that at every moment, I was falling away
from beauty.
In a woman's face I was the eternal coldness,
in her hands the unmaturing child
growing heavier, disturbing her spine
year after year.
I broke my mother.
Going towards what I would not help
the ground unbloomed around me.
One without pain became known
as pain in my fingers, my toes, the wing
of my back.
Time had its own worthiness in which I did not
wait with grace.
I sat in it with death and wrapped life's shreds
like flesh around my hands and from there,
my body.
My invisible body!
There was someone, I remember, who saw it,
who said, dressed as a physician would dress,
'Harvest the falling.'
I replied to that voice with the knowledge
of my wisdom, disclaiming it,
and then was grasped as if a ball caught
at the height of an unknown game.

'Laws That Govern The Stars ...'

after Yasuhiro Yotsumoto

Do not tremble.

Do not listen to wishes falling.

The laws that govern the stars
might offer immense consolation
but it is not our purpose
to be consoled.

Law Of The Gun

'A tiny band of mutineers' –
finger against finger
eye against eye
little adrenalins marching
down the arm
in an army

And now I've got
a bullet in the brain
and it's laughing hard
at the joke about
trajectory

The gun it flew from
was aimed at the heart
but love didn't want to think
about hate

The Laws Of Heaven And Hell

after Silvina Ocampo

1.

The laws of heaven and hell
are repealed and redrawn
at every death.

At the death of a horse
the legislature sits.
At the death of the wheat stalk.

How do you know
that a stone crumbling
does not set the lawmakers bustling?

2.

What is beyond
the reach of these laws
is life.

The two little red-bibbed swallows
on the wire long rotted away
have not given up on eternity.

Unless you have lived forever
your verdict on this
is neither here nor there.

'The Laws That Happiness And Anguish Keep Exchanging'

after César Vallejo
for Rebecca Seiferle

Standing on the wall
you look like some kind
of first idea.
Once you're spotted
there'll be no surprise
at what ensues.
Good or bad.
The apple of your eye
is in your eye.
With the words left over
from what you yelled
from the wall
they're quoting you
elsewhere.
Your lover's trying
to get you down.
They'd rather you died
from a virus
but you don't smile.
You exchanged that
last night
for a stony silence
that today you've
climbed.

There are laws
against everything
in life but those that
happiness and anguish
keep exchanging
are like legs
on a ladder.
One then another.
Up or down.
What you saw
when you weren't
on the wall
certainly is the same
as what you see now
but differently.
Good or bad.
What they're calling
out to you
is what you called
yesterday to some other
silly silhouette.
Far off you spot
the next one.
Far off but looking like
they want to do it
regardless.
You move over
and later you fall.
The wall struts
without ethics.

The Hidden Law

after Auden

There is nothing hidden in an atom, a star, or a human.
Everything is hidden in a word.
A star.
An atom.
The whore's dreams.
The hidden law does not enter a word.
It hides in silence.
Silence is the part of the universe a word cannot do without.
Though a word finds its wholeness when heard.
'Star.'
'Atom.'
'Human.'
Speaking and listening can never find silence.
We are punished by how close they do not come.

The Law Of Hiding
Behind Open Doors In The Dark

the law of those walls
black like mishaps
the law of harm and of tricks
the rules followed by the leaf-mouse
as it blows in a whistle past my feet
the law of the little we have left
of dreams recalled fleetingly
and of moods returning again and again
in search of context

my little child enters this lost place
as if it is a game and laughs
for the length of an average life
moments later I jump out screaming
for her expression
to leave its mark on me forever
like terror thrown
to the bottom of a bucket
and dripping out a jagged hole

her face emptying
her soul to the floor

The Law Of His Grey Sleeve

for Wallace Stevens

Only, his grey sleeve
Redeem us
With your liberty to apply
Redeem
All the good citizens

Only his grey sleeve
In the coherence room
Establishing the facts
And lining them up
Like a dead scream

His grey sleeve
A simple isness
As you might chuckle
As you might
As well

Only his sleeve
Pushed up
So that his hand might work
Abimo pectore
From the bottom of the heart

The Law Of His Knife
And The Laws Of Savouring

after Georges Bataille

Notice
requires excision.
Decision
a certain amount of notice.

His knife had barely touched my flesh
when he could taste me.
It's more a tangle, he said, of my mother's
smell, vigorous sweat and repeat flowers
in the Spring, than of something more
bloodsy, your little ragged blossom
or a loose hanging rage, for
example.

It is, he said, like reading a document
containing not only the oath
of the dead and dying but a soft climbing
up unborn thoughts, the deep-blue ones
that might break the skin and force
no longer a child to the fore of the head,
just under the eclipse taking place
eternally above the brow
that rims the eyes
and sight.

Sort of like snow's cold in Summer or
that Winter sun that people talk about as if
they weren't human but an
advanced plant (not old!) or a flag
that needed drying
in a campaign that stretched
from season
to ugly season.

And his blade was hot, as fire tastes
the animalness of me, and sharpened most
in the moment the heart
was crucial like charity these days
when the tongue can do just about anything
with that heart, make all
things a lie and all truth and even take
a word like responsibility and rinse
it out as if it was a mouth and soap
was abnegation.

He is my leader, my prime minister,
followed if unchosen.
Murder is constantly on my mind… and hope,
like Autumn leaves not leaving, for
as if belief was futile and faith a poultice
for believers, he has involved me
in a process of bleeding for a long time
and for no reason.
Serving up politics eon
after eon: *Let them eat each other.*

Wraith
after pitiful
wraith.

'The Law That Humbles No One'

after Paul Éluard

'Each can read with trust
The law that humbles no one'

The legal mind does not think it
And the legislator does not write it

None can perfect it
Nor can any misinterpret it

For it is a law that doesn't whisper
And a law that does not shout

The law that humbles no one
Is inscribed in the heart that suffers

It says that suffering is a good deal
For only with it can one get past

The right of oneself
To demand justice

The Structural Law Of The Imagination

'this law demands that every image bear witness
for or against the man who imagines it'
IMAGINE war is a structure of immense
and passionate delight or was that a jacobean lily?
with your mouth in the wet grass taste
the unconquerable courage of the sun's rays
imitating almonds in burnt sugar or the knot
of your heart unravelling over this million years
IMAGINE dark hair and complexion breaking
the surface of the argument like a bank of sand
thrown up by the sea or like beauty without
a spectator which prefers to act on its own
see in your mind the low spirits who watch
for grace and divide it at regular intervals
into the specific character proper to the cells
from which it arose or see the cup which caught
his blood like an amphitheatre which could
scoop in the earth as it was lifted toward heaven
IMAGINE a tree crawling along the ground
as a single mourner would towards a forgotten
death and visualize pain as half skin half graft
where what is taken from another brings
with it a mean servility and cartilaginous flap
IMAGINE the insertion of sound within a word
and feigning not to see in a luxuriant
garden planted for the blind and relying
for its impression on nothing the eye can take in
if you can think of a long oval dish for boiling
fish and lie down in it while pretending
it's a five day week and you have but one will

you might understand the amount of motion
required to remain totally immutably still
IMAGINE that you can imagine anything
and then really alive and really dead
the structural law of the imagination sometimes
has the shape of an irregular red blood corpuscle
or a clump or two of soaked sand but odd
and singular and quaint it keeps itself eternally
open to suspicion and quenches any man
who fails to be wary of the heat of his own fire

'The Law Of The Infinite,
Law Of What Has Always Been Empty,
Law Of Hospitality And Silence'

for Edmond Jabès

This, according to who speaks, is the law of the book.
For our words to have value, we must tremble as we write.
And yet we balance like goats on our ideas, interrupt
the sky with our etchings arrowed at civilization
as if they might be what shines out of a dance
and not the sound of a heart, like hundreds of beasts
pawing the ground.

And luck survives… and survives.
The warning, it seems to us, is never about death.
We open its narrative with our hands held before us,
as if magic could execute itself, as if simultaneously
the story was lawful, spontaneous, factory
and a work of art.

We search always for a new cave, empty of other bodies
and think about what is worthy of desire
the way things occur to detectives.
Even beasts have office hearts, all our ideas finally lost
in the argument of infinity.

'The Inmost Law'

for Paul Éluard

In this law you are the mother.
In this law you are the child
In this law you are the father.
In this law you are flesh.
In this law you are bones.
In this law you are a governor
and a slave.
You are nude.
You are clothed.
You have dignity and shame.
In this law you think yourself
and cannot escape yourself
though the inmost law is broken.
Accordingly
to be all
would be to follow it perfectly.
To forget cruelty and kindness.
To forgo your concern.

'The Laws By Which The Irises Rise'

for Maria Buranda

These are those which open the fan of light.
The laws which teach the darlings to recognize themselves.
They say the city was never there.
They tell the star how far to move
    to keep in line with the earth's wobble.
Laws with an axis, they mess hair
    and fossick in the title for a gnat.
In the aged north they listen with their tips
    for the finale of the air.
In the new south they neigh like a tiny horse
    in the vocal chords of a baby.
They are the same piece of music for aeons.
Girl heads.
Such tiny noises and lighter notes.
With a smell like a ladder receiving the sky
    they steal all the forest's breath.
They are the laws which measure the rain's pulse
    and release the sun from its burning virgin prison.
They force the sun's fingers through months
    and spill the moon from its cocoon onto the lakes.
These laws force the little mauves
    into the one-dimensional world of the story.
Whereas the iris has no idea, really, how to recount its life.

'The Irreproachable Laws Of Life'

after Fernando Pessoa

There's pig-meat on my plate again.
If I eat it my cells are replaced.
Replaced and replaced.
Life just keeps attacking me.
Building up as my skin and brain.
Even if I hold still I'm alive.
Even if I'm dead life goes on.
Even where there's no life
life's laws are working away.
Not stopped by boredom or duration.
Steeped in disaster and success.
If I spit the pig-meat out
life's there with an open mouth.
It's appalling and irreproachable.
Not one of its little laws
will ever pass into disuse.
Not one is weakened by a hoot.
They all keep building up
as my toe-nails and liver.
Attacking my motionless desire
to become the pig-meat.
Besailing, assaulting and over-
ruling me.
Steeping me in disaster and success.

The Law Of The Judge
(or 'Cock A Doodle Do!')

The judge of the conspiracy for prizes
for the beautiful arts
in the mining community of nowhere
read and was sure he had read what he read.
At least this time he'd been sensible
and refused to sit on a panel.
Only a lone judge can truly judge!
If there was one thing he hated
it was arguments about beauty.
Especially here in nowhere where
they mined for nothing.
Among all the empty-handed, beauty was so plentiful
that one suspected a god-like conspiracy.
He was, however, an experienced judge
and so tried to put this idea right out of his head.
Tried to clear his head, in fact, but we all know
that can't work if one's skull is an honest bone.
He bent it over the page and went on reading.
With a mechanical little nod he savoured.
He felt almost banausian or as though
he was coming to resemble an optimistic worm.
Any moment now he would push through
and glisteningly soil-covered
announce the outcome!
But he could already hear certain persons
who might or might not be 'experts'
saying he should be investigated.
Not as much as *they* should be investigated
but investigated after all.

Soaring up to his perch on the ceiling
he looked down and decided to offer them
something imaginary.
This thought caused him to spontaneously
utter what made him sound like
a very satisfied old rooster.

The Law Of The Jungle

(i) The Elephant and the Tiger

The elephant went to the jungle
because it was in love with a tiger.
They kissed on the lips.
They had sex but no children.
The tiger's heart was eventually broken
by the elephant's family
which refused to visit.

*(ii) Monkeys (and Other Animals
Which Children Like to Imitate)*

Put your arms
here, make these noises and
walk like that.
Now you have the right
to take your own life.

(iii) Dog Eat Dog

In reality, nothing of substance
has been eaten.
Dogs wouldn't eat this.

(iv) Volcanoes

These are close to the top of the foodchain.

(v) The Jungle

Has a storm
packed in its heart.
The bones of philosophy
are stuck between its teeth.
Fur on a rock.
Zebra light through the trees.
Every broken animal
will never be another word.
There are no traps in this trap.
How did they live there?
They lived.
Like wind inside the rain
beating on a closed window.

The Law Of Kindness

To produce nothing
But yourself
Is the kindest action
For the universe

When pushed
To swing like a little door
That others
May pass through

To be an accident
Of the world
So that even your name
Loses its grip

Like a sleeping cat
In the flowers
You can ignore
The lizard and the bird

How kind is the sun
To those
With enough to do
Just sitting around

How kind
The happiness of cucumbers
And the nest full
With spotty eggs

And as if no more
Than the residue
Of a dream
You might murmur

To produce nothing
But myself
Is all the universe
Expects today

The Last Law

for James Wright

Break the last law he said
And from that moment
Even time became a fugitive,
The bricks cried
To get back to their father's ditch
And tears fell to beg an ocean
To follow behind.

Begin in me he said,
The moment of death
Is the only way
You'll ever live.
Let us all die as people
Awaiting the outcome
Of what we tried.

Leave out angels.
Leave your dead.
We will all get to carry
Bodies on our shoulders
And sing as if it was screaming instead.
Break the last law here,
Where the note is being hit.

Raise your voices
Like a full glass
To the lips of the sky.
Another's dream

Is where your heart is beating
So get started
On what is naked and hidden.

Realizing the error of your ways
Is often like growing
A horn.
Put your head down
And carry on through.
Break the final law
Even if there's only nine minutes left.

The Law Of Law

the gavel

and the idea

what is brought together

and kept apart

the fence

and what's on either side of it

snake in the woods

snake in my heart

if not laughter

what about a tear?

the mother of the fact is the unfortunate truth

whose maiden name is forgotten

we have to give it all up you know

to see the self in the other

executed

home

'The Law Of The Law Of Genre'

for Jacques Derrida & Derek Attridge

as soon as I was born I exceeded my mother
yet implicitly, explicitly, I bore her mark
it was a matter of mention as well as use
I was said to be her child
yet no-one meeting me could tell
it always seemed to me
that I was inside and outside her
at the same time
regardless, it remained impossible
to know who or what she was
and now people remark the same of me
meanwhile, my own children
have sprung from this genre
like abhorrent possibilities
like fascinating, incorrect nodes in my brain
they go off the edges of me
and continue to disturb me
with signals directed to me alone
I create only my own ideas
in order not to notice
they are all being sent to Africa and back
they have the unkempt smell
of unfinished poetry
mother washes them or says they can't belong
I tell her that membership here
is contingent on its lack of determination
she says, I'm your mother

and don't you forget it
remember that the law of the law of genre
was written simply
by some other woman's son

The Wonderful Lawlessness Of God

for Hafiz

Whenever there is a curfew
God is on the street dancing
And if the law says you should be brief
God takes a long time
None of this is because
God is contrary or revolutionary
But simply because
God is no better than the lawmakers
At knowing what's right
And what is wrong
So if you see God
On the other side of the law
Only call softly
God should no more be singled out
Than the rest of us
When it comes to this or that
God is simply wonderfully lawless
And doing God's thing
And when it comes to someone's thing
The law is an ass

The Law Of Life

We live and live and live.
Ash buries us for refusing to become ash.

The Law Of Light

Law glows
Power's inside the thin hot wire
of the sky
written out of theory
In the place where they shone it
darkness got the rut
as if it was a film being made
Now it's soft and a bedroom
and there's right ways
even in the sheets
The lovers are on the hill
because they can see it
from there
The sun cloves and enters
the broth
The little fire
burns out the hesitation

The Law Of The Limit

A limit is neither inside or outside that which it defines.
Margaret Davies

My limits hardly exist
Though at so many moments
They appear to do so.

Briefly, my limit
Is about to scream
But it never does.

For a fraction of a second
It seems (to appear or hide)
But remains beyond hidden.

Inside it and outside it
I congeal
And dissipate.

My limits hardly exist
As all the definitions
Of what they are not.

The Law Of Lips And Keys

after Dylan Thomas

unlocking –
scents underfoot from the disturbed flood of petals;
history from the long white tunnel of tradition;
the round harbour from its nest of vertical glass;
that lip from the celebration of the bite, blood like sap or mercury
      rising;
the laugh from its case of proud humour;
the new old men and women from those young tight skins worn once
and for granted;
those not old from the old;
the wave from the unbidding horizon;
like dervishes the children from their nightmares;
in spirals hungry birds falling to earth;
unlocking unwinding silk of the ocean unfurling on the mirrored
      sand;
transparency from a bleak eye;
the body from the other loosed by sleep;
this story from its telling;
the nesting touch from a passing hand;
the passion that came to be explained from those who come and
      explain it;
that moment when you may be able to say no-one is dying now
by those who have come to save it;
metaphors from their own tight laws and the poets from their small
      moods;
everything from the other and the other the same;
the beach from this small moon;
and horses' hooves from the shallow river –

unlocking

all I put black around the stars, look up at the stars and say, I made
    that

and here in my hand, yellow as a brave egg

there's much more lemon in the lemon than you can imagine

the cloud has a shadow

and the key has been encouraged by a smile on its long visit ...

Little Law

Little law without redemption
Taking a loan to start a new civilization

What you will pay you have already paid
Just like the tree that bears no fruit

The hearts of your children are filled with policemen
Hearts good and bad without exception

Little law against the will of the fruit
What might have grown you already forbade

Laws Of The Lost & Found

When we lose
We find
Justice joins all forms

The Law Of The Love Letter

Upon unfolding
it is easy to see
that in the mansion
of bitterness
and music
they are distributing
tiny cries
Their throats light the way
like one thousand
evanescences
Their lips are flowers
bending like intimacies
toward certain wet eyes
belonging to us

Reading here
has its own dangers
The wind's script disorderly
and on fire over
the bone-ache of the
frozen river
A voice with words which cry
I cannot speak about you
without the betrayal
of a lover
A voice eating words
as first people die
without sugar in their tea
and then later of starvation

The tree
in its morning position
turns away from the face
of this page
The near heart
searches the line
Don't forget Hold me Hold me
for flesh and the soul
But this paper blows wayward
in the flux of love
What does it say
when taken out
on the most hardened
of days?

And what
when you take the mirror
away?
For the preservation
of us both
I read you
over and over
Eyes like eyes
Hands like hands
Hair like hair
My crumbling face
calls my face
and my lungs breathe
like leaves underfoot

It is no metaphor to say
the whole world
is in me
All innocence
All guilt
The letter
and the never-ending flutter
of this emotion
caught in its expression
My dear love
Question me again
and again
I am ready to be judged
by your different heart

A Low Sensible Science
(or 'The Law Of Lovers')

for Peter Goodrich

The low sensible science
Is to determine if in fact
The lovers do love
One another

If in fact
They are in love

It is a science at the level
Of what they are in fact
Prepared to do to
One another

It is a science so low
As to see where the ankles
Of the abyss do cross
So sensible as to never
Wear those sorts
Of shoes

Furthermore furthermore
The results
Of this science
Are always called for
In the courts of love

The results are conclusive
Because all lovers resort
To killing
One another

They always do

The hypothesis being
Proven that love requires
Death or at the very least
Its distinct possibility

The Law Of Lullaby

for Billy Joel

My heart is filled
With the dead.

Dead are in the hearts carried
Like coin in a purse.

They tinkle.
They sing.

The tramp of the tongue
Over history.

Lullabies
To lull the living asleep.

They will sing them
Even after death has taken place.

Though the singer is dead.
Though the sung to.

The ear-witness of love listening
To the everlasting prayer.

Lullaby
Of my heart.

The Law Of Memory & Matter

There is no concrete in memory.
The tulip becomes the beauty of tulips.
Concentration is like the sea.
What part of it washes over you?
Do you recall when the wave became another?
Memory feeds on our belief and disbelief.
If the wind loves the far flower you smell it.
Truth is all feeling.
So don't forget any of the faces of your face.
This way you will know who you are this second.
The little brick that crumbles.
The way the ruin remembers the castle.
More clear than any former inhabitant.
As clear as only evidence can be of what isn't.

The Law Of Months

Learn this, if you keep living
the blunt moans of children when they sleep
the stretch of the nipple
the softness of a dead mother
the twice-used line
the thrice-used heart or coat or cold word

Notice these, if you are alive in Spring
fears of love growing along the fences
wrinkles of love in the skins of the pears
philosophy in the hymn
and the hymen gritty with sand
the constancy of disobedience and its tidy spirit

And if your life goes on and on, month after
month, remark upon
the unpredictabilities
itself and its idea
the raised hand, the court, and the cold wind
synecdoche, the part, the whole

'Laws Of The Motion Of Projectiles
In The Immediate Vicinity Of The Earth'

a poem found in bits & pieces for Arthur Koestler

He said stones rush to earth.
So do ideas.

He said part of their spirit was asking for more light.
Teeth of the sun's attraction.

He said balance and order, not sweet pleasure,
    are the law of the world.
Follow the administrative steps.

He said those who let the scandal leak out
    will be put to death.
We will be blessed and cursed with their heritage.

He said detached bodies would be left behind.
The clouds keep pace.

He said it is not the branch of a tree but a weapon.
Growing from forbidden ground.

He said we are unable to reserve sites
    for Paradise or Hell.
It is a walled-in universe.

He said the apple falls not because of its ripeness
    but due to the motion of the moon.
Reality gradually dissolved between the physicist's hands.

He said the mountain hides the sun at night.
(Before that God was used to extinguish the lights.)

He said no astronomer would be crazy enough
    to publish another astronomer's book.
An aerialist balancing.

He said it is not easy to see how the whole thing works.
Smoke the pipe and sleep in the storm.

He said the oyster-world was full of dynamism
    and imagination.
Now there are instructions for observing the sky.

He said our prayers are a dream dreamt
    through a mystic's ear.
The tramp stars move with a shocking irregularity.

He said they never altered their positions
    relative to each other or to the earth.
Our stained-glass cathedrals fall like petals.

The Law Of The Museum

What got left in the mind
After the rest had left
For the history of the future
Packable into seven large crates
And a shipping container
They're taking it on the road
Bit by bit and insured to the hilt
And just like us
The museum dies like that
Bit by bit and insured to the hilt

The Law Of My Longing

for Leonard Cohen

I sit in my boat on the sand
The sea sounds like wind
and the wind moves sleepily
into any object-made space
Was it tears I wanted
when my face was dry
or the cool tips of your hands
like palms swaying
directly beneath my eyes
or along the broken path
of my longing
And at night I alight
and go back to the palace
to find the bricklayers still shouting
and viewed from the growing wall
the sea inching still further
from my empty sail

'The Mysterious Laws Of Poetry'

after José Lezama Lima

These are really quite unable.
As laws.
As they tend to shy away.
From discovery.
Mystery, you see, is not a prelude.
To anything.
Makes no difference.
If the facts are established.
And poetry.
A deliberate act become random.
If you understand it.
You didn't.
Its mysterious laws preclude.
Anything but.
Wonder.

'The Laws Of The Mystery'

Who shines like the sun, Tattiriya Upanishad?
For thirty-nine years I have lived without scars
and now have put my teeth through the skin!
Shall I eat, be eaten?
At the core of everything is a question
that will not be answered.
Does the rain find its voice on the tin roof
and when the rain speaks on the tin roof what does it say?
When it says the cloud is an anvil is it mistaken?
Why don't you open your mouth, initiate, to answer?
Because you were sworn to silence?
And were you sworn to silence to protect the mystery
or to pretend it?

Now you shine like a sun
welcoming home your dark brothers and sisters.
Remember how they shadowed you
as the scar today has given me a date and from a date,
a memory.
Now I know I have lived!
My belly growls warning God and death
they will not be born.
Tattiriya Upanishad,
I am eaten, I am eating the world.
The laws are devoured and devouring.
Oh wonderful, wonderful, wonderful!
Oh how many gifts do the days give our lives!

The Law Of Nature

Get some
if you can
for art's law
is constant toil
and dead images'
belief is not
in their maker

I'll turn you into a baby!
Look at the stars!
Does drycleaning
have any part
in this?
Get some
if you can

Nature may be
disingenuous
but teasing humans
is better fun
Better fun
than having their guts
for garters

The universe runs
from the point
of every nose
Grass grows
uncuttably

in the cracks
of our reason

Look at the stars
Nature is a ride
with or
without bridges
If the water
can get out
so can we

The Law Of Necessity

Is the smallest law.
It's like a street
that has not yet been laid
on a map.
Or dawn
before it's seen
by the trees of the day.
If you follow it
you will eventually come
to the universe
that passes its laws
in a grain of rice.
If you rest there
you will find
that what is needed is sensible
and insane:
In this space the size
of a maggot,
to live, to howl,
to be silent,
to live for as long as death,
all that's possible
is necessary
and most of what exists here
can be comfortably
discarded.
This law is the smallest.
It's like a little spot
on a spot.

Or the grass
whispering ant-things
to your heart.

The New Laws

for Henri Michaux

We need the poem of God
to talk about these.
For no other reason
do we need God.
How do we speak them?
Some brush stones;
some find space between the lips
in which to make loss
into music; others
get lines and do the original thing
with them.
And when they are ready
to be interpreted by the soul
they are grasped at all their edges
by every little fear and mania
and pulled out of shape
and pulled into shape
and dragged into the future
for a purpose you wouldn't even
imagine.
We say 'These are the new laws
which owing to their beauty
must be followed.
Confusion arises
because you cannot look directly
at them nor understand clearly
their force or meaning.
But be not afraid of doubt:

their alignment
with the desired possibilities
is perfect and their profundity
is equal to how many things
they connect.'
And we need the poem of God
to talk about them.
They are what we are growing into
and the terror they hold for us
is for this thing
we can never name.
How did we make laws
more wondrous than we could obey,
laws so accurate
that they foretold all our efforts
to break them?
For no other reason
do we need God
than our inability
to speak of such things.

The Law Of The Night

'The night, where the law was concerned,
had not yet finished.'

Rodney Hall, *The Last Love Story*

The dark part.
With the law still working.
When collectively the lights of day
    depart.
The night's lights of a different order.
Directed away from evil.
Away from sorrow.
Overburdened.
Holding everything in contempt
    so as to reveal only a closed handful.
Those with a particular purpose.
Or not.
Who we hide from.
Huddle from.
Listen!
Is it the mountain air
    knocking at the door?
It is blown from the lips of the newborn
    coming apart on the rock of their souls.

'Tear her apart' they said
and it was midnight forever.

'Laws Nobody Can Figure Out'

for Juan Gelman

Nobody is clever.
She has deciphered the meaning
of the law by which children die
and all the rest cease to be children.
She fully understands the law
which says we have to have them
(laws) and even comes to my disability
opening out the fecial laws of fairness
and symptomatic negotiation.
Here I draw the line that nobody
has the courage to draw!
Jurisdiction stops at me.
My cause is determined by the law
that cannot be determined
by the law.
My landscape echoes with greetings:
"Our bones are springing from their dust."
"This they do by the law of these very words."
"Nobody who speaks dies forever."

The Law Of Nought

Nought.
Most difficult and most easy.
No ought but no o.
Or at least one short.

The Law Of One

One, and no other figure is the answer to all sums.
                              Stan – creation of Patrick White
                              Patrick White, *The Tree of Man*

We must decide it's all one.
Anything else and we're playing judge.
Mucking about with futility.
This has nothing to do with the priest.
Only with the evidence.
A woman who was a cow for awhile
      is now a goddess.
She has an easy mouth to put lipstick on.
She says it is barbarous
      to keep splitting things in two.
The man into man and boy.
The flower into flower and beauty.
But do you think we listen?
We sit here and watch the figures roll in
      through the door we have opened.
We count for as long as we can.
And as long as we count the questions
      continue being asked.
But in the end there is only the one number.
As far as we get.

The Law Of Outcomes
From The Impossible

a branch went flying
with a bird

there were oranges
on the branch

and in the bird's beak
a tiny knife
to cut the fruit

this is something foretold
for the knife found its place
deep in the heart
of the bird

and the fruit rotted

The Outlaw

I have never had a law.

All laws create me.

The Law Of The Overheard

it is like wrapping an elephant
in your father's words
your mother's tears
they drag themselves off to die together
in the grave of your borrowed heart
always recalling
always weeping
we own no tears of our own
we die in the old old shape
of the others indistinguishable
from ourselves

you come among the bones
and become still
like a small skull resting
inside one larger
and from far far away
hear the sounds of the herd
telling and retelling
and making warm the sorrow
in the thick hide of the living
and as if the living were just tears
in the crying eyes of the dead

they are wiped away

'The Law I Own'

for Lorinc Szabo

The law I own and cannot share
   is your law
      which you own and cannot share

      You and I are bound by this law
      and only *we*
        obey it

The Law Of Parsimony
(or 'The Law Against Getting Laid This Much')

How to unwaste everything.
Take just a little bit?
Say, like Whitman in his diary of the war,
'It is pretty cold', when the ground is frozen.
Or say, as the not-so-pretty wife once said,
we shared-a-man and for the girl it was always like
the parousia, the second coming
of Christ.
Male adulterers are forever getting older.
Who gets younger?
You can't take a razor to time so you see,
it's impossible really,
to waste it.
Or, become accustomed to its passing
as if age is accused only
through its title.
Then, leaving almost all of life for others
might be unselfish or it might
be simply sadly
eyeing the toy of a better player.
Nobody throws seed on hard ground.
Yet all the lovers are now made love to

                                    from a distance...

The end of temptation is in settling
for less.
Willpower shares all the properties of the balloon.

The Laws Of Peace

for Richard de Bury
Bishop of Durham, bn January 24, 1287

The laws of peace
are the same blue
that precedes catastrophe.

The walls of their house
are a bird's wing
ambitious with the nest.

The laws of peace
are obeyed
even by volcanoes.

Even by the dead
as if they were alive
and collecting eggs.

These laws are newborns
conquering heart
after amoured heart.

When war comes
like love
they always surrender.

The Law Of Perception

swanrise
over the water

a fact?
an *impression?*

death's left
bright well

light consuming
its absence

voicewings dis-
appear as sky

God's deciding
whether to be

The Law Of Perfection

How can we live
just this one little life,
confess it, whose idea looms
so much larger, much finer,
more shining, beginning on the way
of devastation, the one long piece
made up of what is short, this conversation,
a talk with exile, how can we live this one life,
laughing among the women carrying water
and crying for the brief love, not knowing
what to do but imagining all things,
all places and times, considering
that accept means take and that the road
drops away just when our feet
are firm?

(How much greater
to do man's bidding than God's
for with God's bidding
no retribution, no responsibility.)

Ask while there is the asking
for in the end the lips are petrified
like the tree lifting its roots
from the outstretched palm
of the soil.

(How great to regret
every action, every thought.)

In his tearing from the earth
a man becomes perfect.

The Law Of The Phrase

A phrase presents at least one universe.
Jean-Francois Lyotard

'Here is the story of...'

Here is the story told only to those
who have been named.
Here is the story of all the silences
which permit this story
to be told.
Any number.
There are any number
of silences.
There is a finite number of sincere gods.
Those who can be trusted
can be counted.
The earth-myths destroy every law.
The little image tumbles and growls
off the tongue.

Here is the story of odd
wrestling with even.
Age of faith...
Love god properly...
Flood, all around this world...
Sumptuary laws...
Blue laws...
As a stone with reference
to the grain...
Leading two, or different
ways...

Time scattered...
A hole in one side...
Like this...
'...obligatory phrases, permitted phrases,
tolerated phrases, prohibited phrases.'
So many lots of form are poured down
that the content never
starts.
Flood, all around this world...
A pond, a drink, a travel, a bath,
a mirage, a drink, a down, an opaque
moment that moves across
the desiring ground...
The question of inklings.

Here is the story of planting
a stake in the waves
of the sea...

One who holds another under.

In the tribunal of possible speech
you too do the phrases
a wrong.
'Everything is as if "language" were not.'
Arbitration drowns
in the throat.

A Physiological Law

As a physiological law, man should be twenty-five,
and woman twenty-three, before marrying.
          D.J. McAdam, *Hints on Writing Love Letters*
          (originally from Thomas E. Hill, *Hill's Manual of*
          Social and Business Forms: A Guide to Correct Writing)

It's not so easy to be man and woman.
To be twenty-three and twenty-five
     or vice versa.
Nor is it easy to marry
     or to do so well.
It is arguably not easy to stay so; nor is it easy
     to unmarry.
Thank Goodness it's easy to be physiological.
To grow and grow.
And rot and rot.
How easy to be unable to escape
     matter; how simple,

                    energy.

How difficult it is to decide anything.
Having fallen in love should we kiss?
Having fallen out of love
     should we marry?
It is arguably lucky that you are twenty-three
     and I am twenty-five.
(Physiologically so.)
Thank Goodness we are sexually compatible.
(Physiologically so.)

How easy it is to grow and grow.

To rot and rot.

How simple.

How simply (physiologically) so.

The Law Of Poetry

he wore the metaphor – hacked through stone in the ages – on his face
when he looked at me and it was stone not like stone, stone
that slipped like flesh to the end and the grave
and then born, eyes closed, then open
firm, for the new falling

through my words I see you:
little hooves, a music box and that dance
Oh, what is it about? and turning to look at himself
sees a woman in a bubble bath with Pablo Neruda wearing
a pink dressing gown that dogs would bark at and his lips traversing lands

of the heart
All this, *makes junction as true*, says Foucault
and that wet poet with the body beneath his hands, in the media of love:
'I can do what I like with these words' (slippery)

Power Laws

Things that obey power laws become less likely
with increasing size according to a characteristic formula.
World Science

And so dictators over thirty foot tall are rare,
Statues of, less so, but then they obey no laws
Unless the laws of birds and salt and wind
Are laws but I know the sparrow carried none,
No laws on its final journey to what was
Remembered by the city, so large that any laws
There had so tired themselves that their only
Chance for survival was to multiply quickly,
To turn into five times themselves or a hundred,
To be more than the winds passing through
Or the salt grains if counting continues with
The flip of each passing hour or day, but then
The city's laws became so numerous, their
Number so large, that they are all the time more
And more unlikely, more unbelievable, like
A cement foot taking a step or a general sleeping
Soundly, dreamless on retreat with a brow
Smoothed by breeze and the shush of birdwing,
Cheeks streaked black with salt's tears as
Around cities crumble according to the smallest
Law, the law of obedience to itself which is found
Untroubled at the core of all that exists and
Which becomes no more or less likely regardless
Of existence, despite dictators and their statues,
Despite the one bird that disobeyed the winds.

The Law Of Prayer

Lose this
the church
hands over the body's place
to write sky
as a token
of grave
or tomb reversing –

Find this
the woman
mistaken for a mother
the man
with head and feet
in the same fear
of ecstasy –

Repeat repeat
soft entering the crumbling
a person is there
releasing –
At last, weeping
lips come in
to the soul

the way love
        dupes the day

The Laws Of The Prison

The 1st law of the prison
Is that you are doomed
To live outside it.

The 2nd law of the prison
Is that inside it you cannot
Live where you live.

The Law Of Prophecy

The end of the week.
These memories.

How many books
have been stopped by war?

Saving seeds
for an imaginary garden.

Remember the smallest thing.
Becoming huge.

The moon divides
and there are two moons.

The night's white bull split
from horn to horn.

It is time for the graceful killing
of certain men.

Those who do not recognize
what cannot be learned.

Might they listen to one
who knows the truth.

About prophecy
and as well what will happen.

The shovel is sharp.
The earth great.

Seedless.
On its knees.

Cloud.
Brother of the mountains, the sea.

Life! What it really is
is more death.

The Law Of Purity

Is this
of the year we didn't live,
what left the background singular
by its death or absence,
of the haunches balanced on
when our bodies understood and acted upon
the laws of watching and waiting?
I've gone into your eyes
with the baby-dive,
with the cow mouth that simply moves,
the day I pretended to be a rock
and found we love the people
who squeeze joy out of stone
because they say our fears
are a rose.
How closely you folded your body
about the thorns and felt metal
as if it was the hundred cries of the leaf.
You came towards the world holding out
a rootless tree, the weight of a white stone
that bore with it a tender moon.
I found your lips opening
into the bloom that would serve as beauty
in our refused empire.
We searched forever
for your natural pupils,
saturated with wreck and fire.

The Law Of Questions Unanswered

for Peter Boyle

These I ask
My friend the poet
And he smiles and tells me
How he writes poetry
With the help of children
From inside the sun
With words he is afraid will die
Too quickly adrift
In the nervous systems
Of others

These I ask
My lover at night
(When I have a lover)
And without turning
He places his hand on my back
Without turning
He is more solid and still
Than any answer
He whispers and I use that sound
For other purposes

These I ask
The I that hides from me
Or is it me
That hides from I?
Long-time traders who met
Sharing money in the womb

Coseismal in matters of love
My doors to the emptiest room
They are certain of my panic
And patient not to answer

These I ask
The world in the form of a day
But a day I choose
Still and in pain
In the tall distance
How many sounds in stone?
Who can afford this life?
Why are our bodies
Untrusted by our laws?
Are we afraid forever?

And my voice
Floods the world
With temptation
And settles here and there
Like a large fly
I am more than two people
Wandering
And lost by my own act
My names now are Angela
Oriana and Perpetua

I know all the things
Which laughter told me
I know that fire and night
Are unforgettable
I am the messenger-
Angel and dawneverlasting

And know the sigh
Within me
Is sighing toward
The sigh within me

Do you understand this?
Do you know why the feast
Is in the home
Of your living reflection?
The one who sees you?
Why your fear of the dark
Is too hard to explain?
What is it you have to do?
That if you understood
It would mean nothing to you?

These I ask
Of the sky I see
With my eyes closed tight
Of the love
Not good enough
Of the parts of me
Living for weeks and years
On nothing
Of the children whose questions
Are always flavoured 'Oh!'

And I am the author
Of these questions
Of the contradiction and gods
Little hates and recognition
That all questions find in me
And my language is whole

In those moments
When I have asked them all
When the answers lose their way
In silence

The Law Of Reality

What are you?

A broken star
inhaling a broken star.

Around you
concrete and trees
continually swap positions.
Love always seems to be
either present or absent.

This has nothing to do
with reality
where the star breathing
sounds like sand
melting into snow.

The Law Of Remorse

for Raimond Gaita

the ghost that haunts you
has its own face

by anything else
you will not be accompanied

people blow me kisses
but the kisses never land

once again I stop and meet
what stops me on the road

these tears
those tears

the gathered clouds
wetting my cheek

and I do not weep most days
but pretend

that I had no hand
in this

the clouds are the ones with the rain
it is the spirit who wakes me at night

and the rain *sounds like* crying
and so do our voices

like prisoners tired
dragged over again that old rough ground

to the house
they never leave

Hello old ghosts!
Hello pretty curtains!

You don't think do you
that I am afraid?

The Law Of The Rubber Glove

There is something rude about a rubber glove.
But is it something you can put your finger on?

The Sacred Law

of the madrigal and the decrees of touch, smell, taste, sight, and hearing,
the desire for justice and sexual desire, the sound of the ocean,
nothing deliberately excluded, a plunge
into unplumbed depths in an access
of ungovernable love
                    Pablo Neruda

Singer, don't mention my body in your song.

My body is sacred.

Sayer, don't say what you remember of me.

Those memories are sacred.

Listener, put aside everything we said.

All those words have been questioned.

Sopherim, writer and counter, close your book.

Its letters are simply anagrams of fear.

The mirror's bell is ringing.

A messenger has come between us.

See yourself cracking into two pieces.

Attraction to what seems a depth.

Flat beautiful death of ground and polished sand.

Watcher, dimensions are for getting buried in.

Do not gaze into desire to find how love gets in.

Taster and toucher, there is nothing for you here.

The salt is bled out.

The noumena are phenomena.

The message is here for us.

Invitation and warning.

Singer, tell the mirror all the secrets.

Those of disappearing perfectly into the self.

Hear the glass glass bell!

Pure justice ringing on the bed of our sea

'The Same Law And Enigma'

after Yasuhiro Yotsumoto

In every universe
is the same law and enigma,
somebody saying
'the same law and enigma'.
It started with a Japanese poet
describing the pattern
of the wallpaper
and continued with a package
thrown onto a train
by an anonymous hand.
I have taken part
by donning
a necklace of thresholds
and writing of ditches
and the moon that grows there.
That you will dream
of strawberries and floods
is next and next
is the same law and enigma
that seeded your dream
in the cloud's throat.
In every universe
is the truth that I wonder
even if I do not exist
though I do not survive
a challenge to this
because no question
survives its answer.

Are you asking me about
the weather?
In Japan it is raining.
A laughing bug
enigmatically receives its drops.

The Law Of The Sea

therockin of the sea
is peaceful is way
is goodman tom
is an unstory story
how many times
the waves the waves
no war is over
the men to home
and the men away

is fail to fail
to confide in the earth
the newyear land
look the last
love the mast
what's done is done
is life undone
the grave of the sea
is still to come

The Law Of Seeing

I have a little eye for everything
A black alabaster eye
A mud eye
A water eye
A whirlwind of eye
The visible come to me
Mushrooms from the darkness
Appearing from disappearance
I close my eye on them
Breaking away from obstacles
Being not

The Law Of Self-Combustion

for Joseph Brodsky

This child is peace
said the fire of the ash

Intimate death
wearing the mask of your sigh

And heat
my forgotten prisoner

Unable to free itself
of this timeless bagatelle

Two stockinged feet
and a bucket of fat

And mystery
undilapidated, unruined

Ghosts smoking
to the cat's contented sound

Up-to-death
not even a spark!

The Law Of Sending, Of Indefinite Address

for Peter Goodrich

I have sent you nothing
Now do you know what I have sent you?

It does have shape
Do you know what shape is the perfect metaphor?

And if it is a sheet of blank paper on this particular day
What might it have said if I had written on it?

We have been in love
Are we still in that same love?

Your actions have changed
Does this mean you are hiding from me?

Your name
Is it a different name?

I call out
Do you recognize what I call?

Over and over until my voice is suffused with the reddest dye
But are you confusing me with a vendor?

I'm selling nothing
That again?

And now I have made the fact that we have a secret public
Is this how the simplicity of a dream is made ambiguous?

I have removed myself from you
In order to love you?

And now you seem a different size and shape from every direction
But am I looking?

No I have chosen to remain with the picture
Can I even imagine a you that is always the same?

A barn I can see from this side or that
Why does it shrink and loom as I come and go?

As nothing is still alone I ask
Are you my relativity?

Steps that need to be taken and are taken
Did I understand that I could never explain?

And what I send
Will it be for you epistolary justice?

What you receive
My unshareable I?

'The Shameless Blessings Of The Law'

after José Lezama Lima

Not really human. Really human.
Hearing the word and allowing it.
Without deviance and disobedience
agreeing on definitions for both.
All laws bless you in their own name.
The shame is yours in being happy
or accursed, in being made or upon.
So don't accept what you do not
for fear of anomie or even anon.
Law is nameless under its name.
And all its blessings theoretical.

The Law Of Silent Things

The failure to provide a ladder
was quite silent in itself
as to the issue of causation.

the silent ladder caught between foot and hand
the grip of the climber in the belly
tightening and loosening the ribbons of betrayal
desire always halfway between things
unmixed, attenuated –

wordless roofs beneath birds' feet, crucifixions
smelling apple blossom, floating on fiddles
playing the angels and the selenites
falling off an evening of gems
into the delicious sky of Summer –

the idea, unfamiliar, not a part of things
unspoken under the stone
free from fine, from open
like the palm of a hand holding immortality
from the consequences of loneliness –

the quiet word like a marble in the ring
dark blue and choking
living and dying at the threshold of victory
gradually collecting the gradual
unmitigated, silently sobbing –

the mirror, eyelike, all we complain about
all that is not said
moving in the soundless ceremony of reflection

having it all done for us
and then renouncing what we have married –

the cup, the hairbrush, the murderer
the jumping cat, anticipation and moths eating
oh, pale mystery –
the solace that comes from uttering the self
and speaking these silent things

The Law Of The Singular Object
That Has As Its Characteristic
That Of Being Only A Law

for Umberto Eco

Tomato. The Law of Comparison.

Soap. The Law of Remembering.

Seed. The Law of Paradox.

Blade. (Grass.) The Law of Simplicity.

Blade. (Knife.) The Law of Identity.

Web. The Law of Multiple Possibilities.

Shadow. The Law of Shedding Skin.

Claw. The Law of Action.

Scar. The Law of Sources.

Moth. The Law of Enslavement.

Tlahuizcalpantecuhtli. Yes.

Recipe & Frame. The Law of No.

Cloud. The Law of Its Form.

Sand. The Law of Forgetting.

Lily. The Law of Belief.

Hole. The Law of Inertia.

Ice. The Law of Dreams Unrecalled.

Soul. The Law of Anatomy.

Penis. (Erect.) The Law of Readiness.

Penis. (Slack.) The Law of Understanding in the Other Direction.

Plum. The Law of Flawless Completion.

Bone. The Law Admitting No Denial.

If shadow, hole and soul are not objects

their laws must become those

which allow for contradiction, influence and recognition

and movement towards attaining the status

of a thing in itself.
Thus, a shadow has more light than the lily
and the hole is sharper and goes deeper
than the knife.
The soul, full of recognition, slips easier than sand or clouds
or melting ice through the minute gaps
in any method.

'The Sky According To Laws'

after Nikola Madzirov

The sky according to laws passed for the protection
of those who are murdered, says nothing.

In this silence the sky invites the stones
to unpile themselves and the birds
to swallow their songs.

The sky doesn't watch and the sky never listens.

There is no news.

That the world is bigger than the earth is not news.

That the little stream could cause a king
to create an army is not news.

That lovers at dawn are monkeys and frogs
at dusk, is not news.

The sky has no sense of them and is their entreaty.

The sky according to laws in force to discipline
the carefree, unhomes anything with a soul.

For this purpose, the sky is unified.

The Law Of The Stars

after Rilke

It is not heart that beats in your body but stars,
fallen there by not falling,
appearing there as summer appears
even if summer be cold.

This is the nature of homecoming: to arrive
with the part of home that was never
a part of home.

To find home always missing the home
you carried in your heart
unless you continually empty your heart
into all you left behind.

For it is true the stars fall and they fall into you!
Feel them, gentle, reposing,
deeply amputated in the infinity of your breast!

The Law Surrounding Fruit From Three Year Old Trees

for Richard and Maya Mohan & the orchard to be

Even without money
we shall buy the children cherries.
They will keep the seeds in their mouths
while they sleep
and every morning we will wake them
after death has taken another day
from their list.
After waking they will follow us
down to the trees
where the man says he is the owner
of the fruit.
How can you own fruit?
They call and he calls back.
He is in love with the rough squat trees
and at night dreams of a marketplace
of grace where the fruit
are more inviting than any church.
There's no god in that apple
he says and passes it into another hand
and the crowds turn away
without offering.
Why do they need flesh that is godless?
Why does he let them take
the fruit of his labour without pay?
When the sun is up
he knows he steals the fruit
from the ground while

behind the hill a bell is ringing.
There has been a wedding.
The children have dipped
their fingers in the earth's blood.
Maybe he kills the dream.
For the trees.
For what they promised him while he slept.

The Law Of Telling It Like It Is

Well, I'm not thinking a damn thing
    that I won't say
It's about time someone pushed the wheel-
    barrow all the way around the house
It's full of little babies waiting
    to be planted
Having no land won't stop us from finding
    something to grow
My tongue stops occasionally and it's always
    purely from fear
Those birds with the enormous beaks
    pick out even the tiniest hoping shoots
Don't worry, I'll tell you you're not suffering
    if I think you're not
There's usually time to apologize and for
    retamping the startled roots
As if there was a normal between us
    I apologize and don't mean it
Always like this as people can't recognize
    which flower's which
Honesty, integrity and truth have similar
    flowers
Growing conditions vary of course
    and their smell is in no way comparable

The Law Of Threes

Come out and say the trick.

Do the trick.

Presenting how great I am.

(Click your fingers
and go back to your life,
balancing
on the narrowest egg.)

The Universal Laws
Of Unnecessary Things

Anything spare.

Anything trained.

Hard facts.

As for judgement:
nothing's right with the sea,
nothing's wrong.

(Corn ripens
without a name.)

The Law Of The Unwritten Law

Magic's magic.
What Gertrude Stein used to weave
the rose that is a rose
and in writing uncast that spell.
Or Mallarmé, patient as one of the alchemists,
dreaming of the book because
aware of what he wasn't able
to accomplish.
Fernando Pessoa states
that there is a law of reason
in the writing of things.
Is it possible this law exists because writers
do not believe?
And so, unwritten, the bone does not decay.
Unwritten, there is no collaboration with death.
Michaux knew this best.
He who leaves no trace, leaves no wound.

The Law Of The Verb, 'To Eat'
(or 'Ménage A Trois In The
Missionary Position')

All individuality 'consumes' itself in culpability.
Derrida on Hegel on Antigone

a sound mind in a sound body
a mind conscious of rectitude
wonderful to tell
and wonderful to see
falls by its own weight
a frightful monster
ill-shapen and huge
and dumb as a fish

nature abhors a vacuum
nature does not make leaps
let him sail to Anticyra
and yield not to misfortune
for necessity has no law
and it is not permitted
to know all things

living eating eating living
a judge of good taste
is like an eagle
that doesn't catch flies
and if I have lost a day
said the Emperor Titus
I have found fifteen foreign phrases
and worked my way
from the egg to the apples

from the beginning
to the end

such a banquet
pops a grape in my mouth
but the law does not concern itself
about very small matters
such as the grape stolen
behind my lips
though without doubt
appetite comes as you eat
property is theft
and it is a fraud
to conceal a fraud!

The Law Of Verification

A difference in the language
allows for what really happened –
more than two hearts
creating among them realistic objects
and the real things sitting between
the words they had chosen
to alert them to the world's insouciance
and the things themselves or how
they might not be that but
some kind of breath going backwards,
universes without need to deny
their collision which in an instant
was the chair in French and der
Stühl in German and a long
history of the object coming to
occupy a different shape
in the mouth as there had to be
the first man ever killed and the tongue,
one day, had to curl or flatten
in a certain way – the past
more particular than any present
no matter how carefully lived
(impossible to live in such a tiny time
as the present) and
what was not understood, la silla
by one and la sedia by another and
a cadeira a cadeira a cadeira
where they all sat in one way
on the same thing which varied
over and over and lived its life

as everything does, imbued,
but then not, really untouchable yet
there, over there, unverifiable
because what is shifts
with the eye, with the ear, with
touch and image in the bubble of the
brain which bursts like the line
around the body at death which happens
sitting and standing and lying
down and from whose variation
is revealed what exists there in truth,
without change, another name for what
remains and what that
certainly is – a sofa!

The Law Of Violent Hands

a torture chamber in my hand
a history of attempts

the hand with a proper name
a form of private sovereignty

a hand coldly silver or dryly wood
hustler aligning the world with horror

the hand writing beside itself
a legacy of other truths

a hand disappearing inside myself
raising another bucket full of suffering

the linedrawing hand
betraying the god of the model

this hand trying to unlearn
in white in black in blank

The Laws Of War

Most of war
is fed by war

~•~

A war is carefree

~•~

We ask war
to justify our weakness

~•~

War ignores totals
because it just keeps counting

~•~

 War protects a frail history

~•~

War, the lover,
adulterer of civilization

~•~

War has green eyes, blue eyes, brown eyes
We bequeath these eyes to our children

~•~

War teaches us
that all justification is mistaken

~•~

If you hide a war in your heart
the war will be waiting for someone to find it

~•~

Even a war everyone expects
takes the dead by surprise

~•~

War has no desire to harm
those purple flowers

It forgets its own desires
whilst fulfilling those of men

~•~

War makes love stronger

Do you want your love
to grow that way?

~•~

Your son falls in a war
and though, in truth, some sons live,
none get up

~•~

Spell war backwards

Then let the idea cook awhile

~•~

Wars laugh
at all Laws of War

In action
become Divine

The Law Of War On Television

Exchanging war for the signs of war.
                    Jean Baudrillard

War in houses, in homes.

What happens like this?

Such a small space to accommodate such massive
failure.

The immensity of the heart.

Torn. Adrift. Only close
to the earth it is already touching.

The house is a grave
for a moment after this lifetime of work.

Hear their footsteps enter the heart.

They were willing to go so far
as if bravery wasn't a last resort.

How do things happen like this? Where did this
begin?

Is there a name for the journey of a single drop
of water as it begins in the cloud
and then falls as rain?

What happened, happened.

Yes, but we shall never say out loud
the real war.

Their excuses are bombs.

On the screen the soldier is just someone
like god.

Our homes are what you switch off.

The Law Of Water

To know the laws is not to know their words,
but their power and force.

           Celcus, Consul in ancient Rome
           1 *The Digest of Justinian* 20
           Charles Henry Monroe trans., 1904

I photocopied the ocean and it came out
black and white

I wrote about it and it dried
on the paper

If I threw it down and walked
over it

It sounded gritty like sand in the quietness
of a deserted beach

Where like a woman for all seasons
I cupped my hands

Hostages of hope around the water
of justice

Which trickled despite all oaths and
despite all oaths ran

What is
the law of water?

What is
prophecy?

The deepness of language
and the blindness of the diver

Who does not know which way
is up

Living underwater the pink and red
mollusc of my heart

Hears its own arid beating drown
on the page

Law Of A Watermelon

proof, when it decays,
foretells the past
which the future was tortured
to admit

there I arrive
with hundreds of pages
which do little to convince them
of a watermelon
the sole cause of a summer's day
in deep autumn

there is a wind, too,
with the terror of a thousand
screaming trees
not felt or heard
by the sweetness dripping
through our fingers
to our knees

contentment
is just this way and still,
as all is left unfinished,
the satiety of a single being
will not be proven

The Law Of What?

memo: stranger in the building
there is a man among us
dressed in overalls
asking for money
so that he may go home
give him nothing
he lives nowhere
his hands move like goldfish tails
he drinks cognac from the lampshade
his arm is like a black loaf of bread
he is the theft of this
long time that has in it a true story
and what if you think Hitler good looking
is there a problem with that?
and does anyone know what this man looks like?
the quiet unfamous evil
that is insufficient
but try anyway

The Law Of What Cannot Be Eluded

between Whitman

The law of the past cannot be eluded,
ask those born with their hair already grey.

The law of the present and future cannot be eluded,
just ask the answer.

The law of the living cannot be eluded ...
life might fall and fall but never hits the bottom, simply becomes
    death
with its infinous ability to transfer.

The law of promotion and transformation cannot be eluded,
simply consider.

The law of heroes and good-doers cannot be eluded,
you go by one name, you go by two, beneath the cloud that makes the
    earth
quake, your names also break, with what great patience
they break and reform.

The law of drunkards and informers and mean persons cannot be
    eluded.
The drunks lick out their own insides while the world spins
oblivious to the secrets stolen and the secrets made
by all fellows.

So much cannot be eluded that what can is easily missed.
Like the law of fluff,

the law of the little pink stone that resembles another
or the law of relevance.

But the really interesting thing about laws is the way they come
    packed
inside each other like Chinese boxes.

What cannot be eluded are the laws of opening and the laws
of closing and how these are joined, how flux
stays the same and how what happens
is a law unto itself.

The Law Of What Does Not Exist

The whore does not exist.
The soldier does not exist.
Style does not exist.
Being dead does not exist.
Now does not exist.
If you have feet
    your feet exist;
        if you have hands
            your hands exist.
The law governing
    what does not exist
        applies to hands
            and feet.

The whore and the soldier sit
over a drink
and a man thinks
she's dressed like a whore
and a woman admires
the soldier's uniform.
    Hands touch hands
        and feet
            touch feet.
The law governing
    what does not exist
        applies to touching
            and feeling.

The whore does not exist.
The soldier does not exist.
Wildness does not exist.
Nor does another's pain.
Loving is wild.
Being dead is not tame.
    Teeth and claws exist;
        if you have teeth
           and claws.
The law governing
   what does not exist
      applies to teeth
        and claws.

Everything that does not exist
exists in another form.
The whore
is a white leopard.
The soldier is the jungle
at night.
    Her feet
       make no sound
         on his path.
The law governing
   what does not exist
      applies to sound
        and silence.

Soundlessly she takes
him apart with her claws.
Screaming he comes
apart in her claws.

Now exists.
Death exists.
   He does not fight.
      Whatever he offered
        was not enough.
The law governing
   what does not exist
      applies to soldiers
      and whores.

The Law Of What Ensues

Three times in the history of the world
mystery turned its borders inward.

And there the thought as if it was God's thought;
and God's hollowed head;
and the head as if made whole by its thoughts.

What then ensued three times
 the loss of eyes, mouths, ears
     days, months, years

our own voice in the blind return
not surviving its emptying

chaos smelling like the sauntering earth.

(Laws Of) What Haunts

what haunts is also a haunt
Avital Ronell

Unhomed, finds its ghostliness,
Absentless, lacuna in the lasso,
Bringbacking, the ever-attached,
Atomy, walking the dead,
Irruinible, armgaunt and leggaunt,
Unplayable, deadborn double,
Placeless, life-denied and tomb-lifted,
Suddening, the time-forbidden,
Without, without without without,
Haunting, and becoming the haunt,
Nothing, that is something terrible,
Mistake, that is wrong,
Habiter, less and more than the living,
Grin, not fitted with teeth.

The Law Of What We Call Laughter And Is In Fact The Wound

for Kate Hulme

And so, laughter grows its theory around the wound.
It is like this the dragon came to history.
Like this that poems grew up around the stars
and fixed them in the sky.
Laughter is a sound like leaves,
painting the whole of the body
with long multiplication, the homework of grief.
The opulent lattice of evolution, time refining mystery,
allows it entry to the shell-canal of sound,
to earmark the veins with large sighs and tiny bubbles.
Fear whispers here behind curtains of redemption –
Blue couch, library of creature-sheathed signs,
secondhand joy, lightning flash in the trill
and castaway of busted memory!
And finally, eyes clothed and seething tears.
Silent laughter as the universe shakes its mist to a puddle
on the tyrant's floor – the contradiction of I!
Bone that unites with soil.
Struggle of the fruit towards its seed.
From table to table, how amusing the sad hole
at the centre of each plate.

The Law When There Was No Law At All

Where the memory of men did not run
there was no law.
                    David Mellinkoff

When there was no law
we do not remember.

In all that's forgotten
there is no law.

We fall into lawlessness
when abandoned to the past.

It is only in the future
that there's no law at all.

Now is the time
we are eternally bound.

Law is the memory
we allow and disobey.

What we do not remember
is subject to nothing.

The Law Of Wind

somewhere
the place of birth of that wind
insisting on windy days
I write about wind
keen scent prancing
through the confidence of uncut grass
disordering the sensitivity
of the still swing
that has unmeasured flesh
until it fits the sky
bothered by all it touches
everything restless and equivocal
hot and then cold
on a day for marriage
it unscrupulously confuses a crowd
which huddles pallid
as a whale in this park
a pair of pink fairy wings
flies into a tree
and clutched flowers
pilgrims of the pale sun
turn their heads to the sound
of a child crying
three hundred leaves suddenly falling
create a false sense of excitement
and a beautiful girl laughs
inside its wandering hands
sleepwalking that night
she whispers
to the wind still whispering

kicking at that other body
moving inside paralysis
feeling its wanton
rackety breath
its teeth on the back of her neck

in this dream I am satisfied
nothing matters

The Law Of Wine

Is not in the grape
or the earth
in the nose or time
or beauty of words
unable to describe the wine
but in cracking the heart loose
at its edges
just enough to let sunlight
beneath its serious face
to illuminate the smile within
the glass's umbrous curve
the little bit of rest
that moves us towards chaos
and acceptance
towards the slight opening
in the clenched world.

The Law Of Witnessing

He told me he saw the tree trunks
    turning to water, that his hand
        covered with soil was a damp
            stone.

He told me he saw these things
    with his living eyes and that when
        he had no eyes he still witnessed
            his life.

He told me there is a Law of the Motion
    of Heavenly Bodies and another, hidden,
        of Gravity in History.

There was a man, he said, who in order
    to be King had to kill everyone from where
        he came.

Everything shall only be possible once, he said,
    and I am a chronic condition, submissive
        to the blood and the remembered
            star.

The Law Of Wood

I have my hand against this
and it is like skin
but does not make me weep
like skin
and does not make me
remember passion
but love life
even devoid of passion
and prepare that fire
for death.

And wood
contains as many rivers
and trees and stories
as the cloud and earth
from which it grew.
Its eye
within my eye
is discerning every
duration.

With my fist I knock on it
and hear
its fatal voice.
Never whispering.
Always clear.

Some Of The Laws Of Words

The torrent of words
is carried forward
by silence

~•~

The word is never safe

Once hands
rivalled the tongue

~•~

There is nothing before the word
that pertains to the word

~•~

The contagion of speech
is caused by what matters

~•~

Words are the tongue
doing theory

~•~

Words lost
amid the important lives
of punctuation

~•~

No dog is at the mercy of language
No dog has a throat that commits things

~•~

All words we say contain shades
of exclamation

and greeting!

~•~

Everything we say reminds us

of boredom and loneliness

~•~

Words are our convenient desire

They accuse us of the effort
of being ourselves

The Law Of The World

The world is not preparing
to map the lands of my desire

It is planning another country
in which to rest my heart

Why this strange seed
that will bear no native fruit?

Why wine poured from my mouth
into a foreign cup?

My love recognizes all
that is familiar and not

So how can the world insist
on this closet of riches and dust?

Hearts must walk trails hot and soiled
by the trials of many feet

But all paths
are the one path

There is only this world
to turn its back on you

Leaving itself
because love is hard

The Law Of The Wound

Is a wound still a wound
on a dead body?

Does it straddle the enormous distance
between death and dead?

In 1946 at the King David Hotel in Jerusalem
seven churns together

made one whole man
a complete bomb.

It is said here of the dead
that no bodies remained

but wounds were many.

One wound stretched from a beautiful woman's idea
twenty years ago about loving a man

to the last moment she glanced
at her daughter's face.

At breakfast.
Now it is night

and those wounds sent out fifty-seven years ago
to wander

are still fresh on the water
and bread of the world.

A wound never remains on a dead body.
It migrates to a heart that remembers it

and feeds it.

The Law Of Writing

Is that of reading death.
Its literal, unavoidable text.
Written if only written virtually.
Addressed to each of us personally.
Obey the word insofar as it is desirable
                           to become known.
Remembering that in each and every word
                          the word's end is sown.
Relinquish language to its record and your breath
                              to the not yet spoken.
For writing's law decrees that when any word is read
                            the dead are woken.

The Law Of 'X'

marks this spot

what happens when perception
is sharpened to breaking point

variable

The Law Of Yes & The Law Of No

Yes has none.
No is one.

The Laws Of 'Yesterday & Tomorrow'

The event
bears upon its future
and its past
like a bucket of water
splashing
before and behind
the feet of its carrier.

There was
and will be no justice
like this love
in the muscle and stride
giving
the earth reason to believe
in the present.

A little
earlier or a little later
and he would not
have seen her on the balcony
alone
and walked away
without saying his heart.

There was
and will be no today
like this love
in only its loving
holding

what's been and gone
in the arms of now.

How warm
is the embrace of yesterday
and tomorrow
and how the universe
cannot help
but begin again each instant
such a clasp is given.

The Law Of Zero-Grazing

From this moment on,
this precise moment,
the exact time or zero hour
fixed for the beginning
of this practice,
everything will be delivered.

Cut grass, acts of hope,
sticks and fine sand.
Stamping of the heels,
a ribbon or fillet, flocks.

If for any reason,
any reason at all,
there is a need to go out
from this moment on,
the earth will waver
and simply fall away.

Do not be irresponsible
and responsible for this
but wait for what is brought.
Notices, rippling water,
a baker's grater?

Whatever they bring
will have no unfortunate
consequences surely,
for it must be assumed
it was not needed elsewhere?

A grim, a tidy, a bottle
of hay, what happens
when one person
chooses another.

The Law Of ZZZZZZZ
(What There Is Not Time For)

Often talked about as if it was a kind of sleep,
is the list unwritten when the day comes,
what there is not time for and will never be:
shovelling water, carefully folding back
the house to reveal the face, the sea ascending
like voices of the sun, hope most often felt
when there is none, every possibility of your-
self — black head like the rock ready to receive
the snow; golden head of the gentle bird
rising through the earth, leaves and pebbles
and cold flesh where the star was, the body's
lightning scraping at the bones for sense,
The Law of Answers, The Law of Brides who
leave on ships with bowls of oranges in their
slender arms, The Law of Little Hates and
The Law of Coherence.

And we were meant to learn love from our
mothers' torsos yet all we learned was haircuts,
sunglasses, The Laws of Jesus and Some Other
Bold People, false promising, enslavement and
finally, forgetting. All our life, perfectly unable,
and now our lives list to the side where the first
moment beckons us back through The Law
of Old Toys to become the last and eternally
reminded child, to follow along a darkening sky
The Law of the Little Bird Full on Crumbs,
to clumsily descend the ladder leaning against

The Law of Hazard and to walk, as if our legs
still could carry us, into the chambers and valves
of the heart.

At last, silence! Despite The Law of Things
Which Speak. This is the place where each and
every inhabitant is bound by The Law of Writing
Poetry in Collaboration with Poets Dead. Here,
it is impossible to kick one's toe. Here, they
build no toe hospitals. Here, they pass no toe
laws. There might be ears but they are not used
for listening. There might be hands but they
are not used for clasping. There might be be-
ginners but they follow immediately The Law
of the Progressive Decline of Beginning. Here,
is where is learned the enormous gift given by
contradiction — relief! And so is seen the true
glimpse of eternity. It resides between your
stomach and your chest and lives its life eating
away at all things.

All things. The Laws of Populations. The Laws
of the Disingenuous. The Law of Eggs and of
Salt. The Law of Bindings on the Wrists and the
Ankles. The Laws of the Passional, The Laws
of Oracles, The Law of Goodwill and The Law
of Thought Thinking Itself. To some end we
thought for far too long and now are released by
The Law of Imaginary Causes into not so harsh
a place for when we turn our back on The Law

of This Illness it invites no prayer of recovery
but sits as if poured into silence – a hurricane
of stillness with little or no hue, its outline the im-
penetrable hybrid of our indefinite shadow
and false shape.

Postscriptive Law

The law says you must die.

And then you die again.

Acknowledgements

Agenda (UK); *Alternative Law Journal; Anemone Sidecar* (e-anthology, Ravenna Press, USA, 2004); *Ant Ant Ant Ant Ant* (USA); *Arquitrave* (Colombia); *ars poetica; ars poetica* (USA); *Australian Humanities Review; Blackacre; Breaking Free* (Central Texas Live Poets Society Anthology, USA, 1998); *Cardozo Studies in Law and Literature* (USA); *Electric Acorn* (Republic of Ireland); *Equinox* (UK); *Famous Reporter; Four W; Green Integer Review* (USA); *Green Left; Hermes; Hobo; Hoisted; Human Rights Defender; Hutt; Imago; Island; Jacket; kritya* (India); *Law and Literature* (USA); *Law/Text/Culture; Legal Studies Forum* (USA); *Litter* (UK); *Mascara; Meanjin; Mike & Dale's Younger Poets* (USA); *Newtown Bridge; Open Boat – Barbed Wire Sky ~ Poems for Refugees* (Live Poets, Sydney, 2003*); Out of Sight, Out of Mind: Prose and poetry about the prison* (The Bridge Foundation, Ginninderra Press, Canberra, 2005); *Pandora's Box; papertiger; Pixel Papers; Pemmican* (USA); *Poems Niederngasse* (Switzerland); *Raunchland* (UK); *Retort; Romancing the Tomes: Popular Culture, Law & Feminism* (Margaret Thornton, ed., Cavendish, London, UK, 2002); *Salt River Review* (USA); *Sawbuck* (USA); *scarp; Shampoo* (USA); *Shearsman* (UK); *Short Fuse ~ The Global Anthology of New Fusion Poetry* (Rattapallax Press, New York, USA, 2002); *Shot Glass Poems,* (Caffeine, Anthology of Short Fictions, USA); *Sidereality* (USA); *Slope* (USA); *Small Suburban Crimes* (UTS Anthology, 1999); *Snow Monkey* (USA); *Stylus; Tasmanian Poetry Festival Anthology, 1998; Templates for Activism* (Canada Council for the Arts, Ottawa, Canada, 2002); *Text; The Age; The Ardent Sun; The Australian; The Australian's Review of Books; The Best Australian Poems 2003* (Peter Craven, ed., Black Inc., 2003); *The Best Australian Poems 2004* (Les Murray, ed., Black Inc., 2004); *The Canberra Times; The Manhattan Review* (USA); *Three Candles* (USA); *Thylazine* (and *Thylazine's Poets for Peace*); *Time's Collision with the Tongue* (Newcastle Prize Anthology, 2001); *Tool, A Magazine* (USA); *Verandah;* and *Yale Journal of Law and Feminism* (USA).

'The Law of Descriptions', 'The Law of Ducks', 'The Law of Blue Eyes', 'The Law of Hiding Behind Open Doors in the Dark', 'The Law of Water' and 'The Law of Concrete' were published in *Everything Holy*, Balcones International Press, Temple, Texas, USA, 1998.

'The Law of Wine' was published in the book, *Poets on Drugs* (kellyryan press, 2003) and performed at the exhibition *Drugs: A Social History*, held at the Justice & Police Museum, Sydney, 2003, as part of an *ekphrasis* project by the group DiVerse.

'The Law of Nature' and 'The Law of the World' were published in an e-booklet, *4 From 4 Does Not Equal Zero, Poetic Inhalation*, USA, 2004).

'The Law of Absolutes', 'The Law of Crimes', 'The Law of Kindness', 'The Law of the Love Letter', 'The Law of Necessity', 'The Law of Wine' and 'The Law of the Wound' were published in *The Ridiculous Shape of Longing ~ New & Selected Poems*, Cultural Institution Blesok, Skopje, Republic of Macedonia, 2005 (Macedonian/English edition).

'Power Laws' was shortlisted for the *Rosemary Dobson Award*, ACT Poetry Prize, 2010.

The author would like to thank the Literature Board of the Australia Council for a New Work Grant which was of great assistance in the writing of this book.